The Grace and Kindness of Words

A Book of Words, Positive Affirmations, and Happy Thoughts.

by

Niki Nicoletti

Balboa Press books may be ordered through booksellers or by contacting:

Balboa Press
A Division of Hay House
1663 Liberty Drive
Bloomington, IN 47403
www.balboapress.com
1 (877) 407-4847

Because of the dynamic nature of the Internet, any web addresses or links contained in this book may have changed since publication and may no longer be valid. The views expressed in this work are solely those of the author and do not necessarily reflect the views of the publisher, and the publisher hereby disclaims any responsibility for them.

Any people depicted in stock imagery provided by Thinkstock are models, and such images are being used for illustrative purposes only.
Certain stock imagery © Thinkstock.

ISBN: 978-1-5043-4491-3 (sc)
ISBN: 978-1-5043-4492-0 (e)

Library of Congress Control Number: 2015918773

Print information available on the last page.

Balboa Press rev. date: 1/14/2016

BALBOA.
PRESS
A DIVISION OF HAY HOUSE

To my parents who opened my eyes to the beauty of the world.

To my husband Mondo who pushed me to reach for the stars.

I love you.

Preface

I've always loved words. My favorite thing about them is how a single word can evoke so many emotions. I love dissecting and deconstructing words. I love that words tug at your heart strings. Words can elevate and motivate you to reach for the stars. They can serve as a warm blanket on a cold and rainy day.

I've always written poetry and short stories but I've always struggled with sharing my work with others. Many times I've begun writing a short story or novel and never finished it. I would create poems but never share them with anyone. I've felt stuck and afraid to share my thoughts with the world.

I've chosen to write this book for you because I want to share the beauty I found when I truly discovered the magic of words. I've spent years giving friends and family members rocks and tokens engraved with the word "dream" or "believe." The raw and unplanned emotional reaction they shared when they received my gift was so rewarding. This truly created the bond and appreciation I have for words. I've learned what power a simple word can have on each of us.

As I played with some of my favorite words I realized I could create many new stories and experiences. Writing this book has increased my own level of happiness. As I expanded the life force of each word I gained more gratitude and appreciation for my own life.

I hope you enjoy the play on words found in this book. I hope you feel inspired to create your own story.

Wishing you good health, happiness and a life filled with LOVE.

Niki

Dedication

I would like to dedicate each word found in this book to all my fellow humans who are suffering and battling with the will to live and have contemplated leaving this world too early. The suffering created by the power of words can often be unbearable and the only feeling dominating the heart is hopelessness.

This book has been written as a way to remind us all that what we say, the words we choose to use, can often be more powerful than the actions we take. The effects of our cruel, verbal expression can damage another's soul far beyond anything comprehensible.

Be gentle and kind when you judge another person's choices. We should work towards elevating each other rather than tearing each other down.

I send my sincere apologies to anyone who has felt the effects of a cruel word or statement. I dedicate this book to you because the goal is to celebrate your uniqueness and your inner beauty.

With much LOVE.

YOU are AMAZING

Artistic. Mindful. Alluring. Zestful. Intelligent. Noble. Gorgeous.

love….

let oneself victoriously emerge

DARE to be yourself...

Dream. Act. Reach. Engage.

HOPE

Hearts Optimistically Playing Endlessly

boldly express love.

indulge.

explore.

vibrantly encourage.

BELIEVE

Travel to Idyllic places.

Create memories that are everlasting.

"FAMILY"

Fun   Affectionate   Magical

Imperfect   Loyal   Yourself

"Smile"

My dog Melon makes me smile.

What makes you smile?

Search
Openly
Understand
Limitlessly

"Soul"

Dog ...

Dedicated

Obedient

Giving

"I'll love you to the moon and back"

Cat...

Charismatic

Aristocratic

Temperamental

"Because I can"

Freedom

Forging, Risking,

Evolving, Embracing,

Discovering, Observing,

Mastering.

"All Humans Are Created Equal"

Fear is an emotion that awakens your senses. Its special power can help you climb your own personal Mount Everest. It fuels your courage. At first sight it's mistaken as your enemy but soon you realize fear is more of a friend. Fear pushes you beyond your capabilities. Fear opens your eyes to what you've been missing. It pokes at you hoping it will come face to face with the fierce warrior living inside of you; anxiously awaiting the battle to begin. Fear ignites the flame of determination. Fear is uncomfortable. Fear is hated and loved all in one breath. Although fear seems powerful and indestructible it is weak when compared to the grit and bravery of your spirit. Fear is clueless to the outcome. You will reign victorious.

Fear, this message is filled with sincere gratitude and appreciation. You push me beyond my limits and with this effort on your part I am able to accomplish great things.

Victory

An Outcome based on one's efforts to...

Validate. Inspire. Caress. Teach. Offer. Rely. Yield

PURE

People United Risking Everything

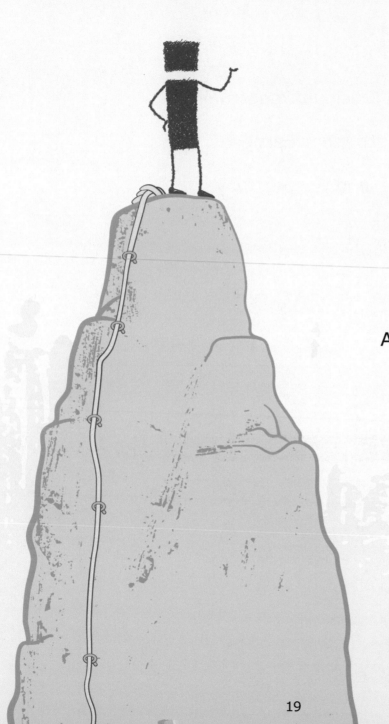

Declare

Radiate

Embark

Aspire

Maximize

Always DREAM Big.

A Precious Opportunity

to Work Earnestly

and Respectfully

Power

F. Fascinating

U. Unimaginable

N. Nonsense

Life...

Limitless, Intentional, Fantastic, Essential

You grace the room and that
moment is magical.

You are.....

Gentle. Remarkable. Admirable.
Caring. Engaging.

FAITH

Fortitude   Anchor   Identity   Tolerance   Humility

A friend is someone you treasure.

You are rewarded with their kindness.

It feels like you are living in a state of utopia.

It's a sacred relationship.

Be thoughtful when it comes to their heart.

Trust

Horseplay and Pajama Parties = Youthfulness

'Happy'

You are **STRONG**.

You **Speak** with confidence.

You **Tell** the truth.

You **Respect** others.

You have an **Open** heart.

You **Nourish** the soul.

You are **Giving.**

STRIVE

The spark in your eye tells the world that you are tenacious and firm in your resolve. You possess a strong intuition that should never go unnoticed. When faced with challenges your wisdom and valor are the driving emotions that protect those nearest to you.

Always lead with confidence and with your heart.

Courage

Countless Obstacles.

Unwavering Risk.

Astonishing Grit.

Excellence.

When we cherish others we create harmony within our environment.

Connect, Honor,

Encourage, Recognize,

Improve, Serve,

Hug.

LAUGH

Life Always Unleashes Great Humans.

Forgive

The beauty of a rainbow

lies in the release

of a wounded heart.

Balance.

Beginning a life and navigating carefully = evolution

You may be asked to step forth and lead

Or sit back and learn.

Both require effort.

Don't allow yourself to only smell

that which is disturbing.

Be caught off guard

by the Poet's Jasmine.

Awareness

Walls are the judgements we place on ourselves.

We are worthy of receiving and accepting our infinite potential.

Removing the walls eliminates all limitations.

Welcome all of Life's Love and Smiles

-Because-

Be the Cause.....

Be – "cause"

"Create Aspirations that are Unlimited and Support your Essence"

Sound connects all continents, all people, all species, all races,

all religions, all political views, all orientations, and all languages.

It becomes the common universal emotion.

There are no limits, no boundaries, no explanations needed.

There is either a surge of laughter or a wave of tears.

Both cause the heart to flutter.

The song of a bird needs no interpretation.

It needs no translation.

It is universal.

This is the gift of Music.

Our thoughts determine what we bring to the table.

Our thoughts determine our attitude.

Our thoughts allow us to show up.

Our thoughts navigate our ship.

Our thoughts lead the way.

You have unlimited potential.

Be the sugar in someone's coffee.

Be the honey in someone's tea.

Harmony

40

People Universally Respecting People

with Open-mindedness and Sincerity

and without Exploitation.

-Purpose-

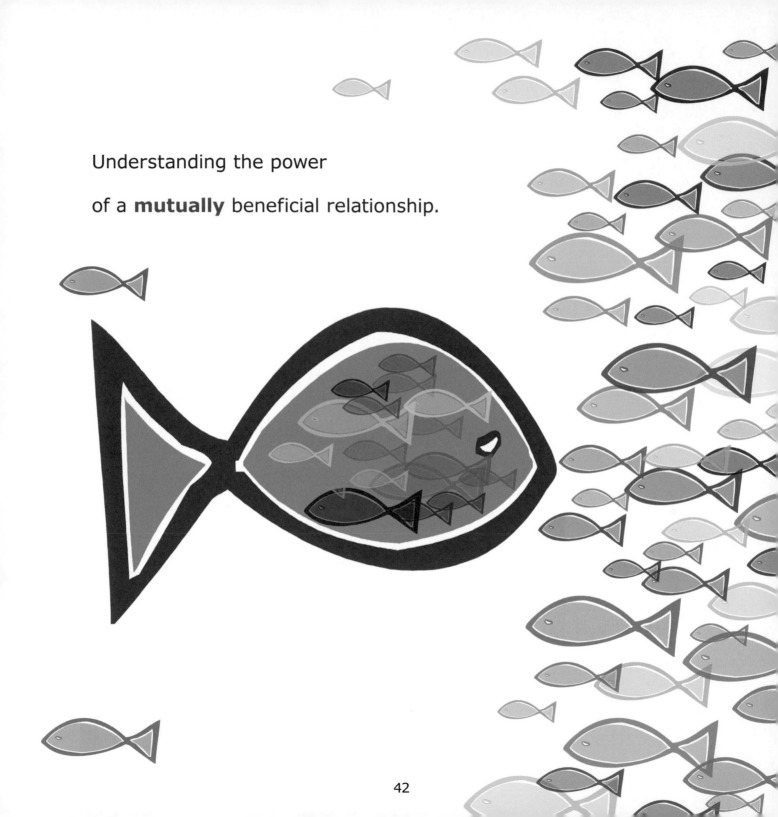

Understanding the power

of a **mutually** beneficial relationship.

Butterflies are **E**nchanting.

Awaiting the arrival of a **U**nicorn..... **T**hrilling.

Yodeling.... music to my ears.

So many ways to define beauty.

The gift of a **freckle**.

Anyone lucky enough to have a beautiful **freckle** is beyond special.

What a unique gift.

The characteristic and personality of a **freckle** is so distinctive.

Only a select group of people are rewarded with such a prize.

If you are one of the few charmed people who gets to sport a **freckle**

please know you are coveted by many.

We love your **freckles**.

They are beautiful.

Be boastful as you rock them!

Allow yourself to **FALL** for ...

Possibilities.   Experiences.

Adventures.   Happiness.

I Declare.

You Beware.

My Best Self is being unleashed.

Windows of opportunity are often small.

We blink...and the moment may be gone.

The unknown can feel like a dangerous place.

A slightly elevated heart rate created by

anticipation and eagerness ignite a flame deep inside.

To serve the world with your gifts

A most stimulating and invigorating

experience.

Launch your ship.

Embracing the morning allows you to create a plan for your new day.

Occupy yourself with work that you love.

Take a few moments to reflect on the effects of your actions and how they will influence others.

Be mindful when responding to unexpected challenges.

Take charge of your life by not reacting but rather reflecting.

If you are unsure of how to handle a situation that arises, ask for help.

Be purposeful not forceful.

Challenge yourself to work towards the betterment of your community which ultimately will benefit humanity.

Empowerment = Self Discovery

Empowerment = People helping People.

Each day I am born.

I celebrate my breath. I am granted the opportunity to become happy. I am surrounded with the natural beauty of our planet. I am gifted with the ability to choose the outcome of each day. When I am faced with unexpected hurdles I am free to decide my attitude and devotion to resolving challenges. I am the luckiest human alive. I can enjoy the silence or choose to live in the chaos. I can delight in full contemplation. My insecurities may creep up on me, planting seeds of doubt but when I yield, and look both ways, I realize I hold the key.

This is my prayer.

"Time is an instant, a moment that can't be replaced"

The blank journal pages that follow have been included in this book for your enjoyment.

They are an open, creative space for you to begin your own journey of exploring and creating new extraordinary words.

As we often hear – our life is truly a blank canvas. The colors that become a part of our journey are defined by our experiences, our joys, and our dreams.

Words can add color and meaning to our hearts.

Join the Movement.

Become your own Word Advocate!

Journal Notes

Journal Notes

Printed in the United States
By Bookmasters